Eli Whitney

Cotton Gin Genius

Kaye Patchett

BLACKBIRCH™
PRESS

THOMSON

GALE

San Diego • Detroit • New York • San Francisco • Cleveland
New Haven, Conn. • Waterville, Maine • London • Munich

THOMSON

GALE

For more information, contact
The Gale Group, Inc.
27500 Drake Rd.
Farmington Hills, MI 48331-3535
Or you can visit our Internet site at http://www.gale.com

Photo Credits: cover, © Blackbirch Archives; pages 5, 8, 9, 15, 17, 20, 22, 29, 39, 42, 44, 57 © North Wind Picture Archives; pages 4, 7, 40 © CORBIS; pages 12, 25, 27 © Bettmann / CORBIS; page 14, 51 © Francis G. Mayer/CORBIS; page 34 © Phil Schermeister/CORBIS; pages 11, 18 © Photo Disc; page 26 © National Archives; pages 31, 32, 58-59 © Hulton|Archive/Getty Images; pages 35, 36, 45, 48 © Library of Congress; page 47 © National Portrait Gallery, Smithsonian Institution/Art Resource; page 54 © Dover

LIBRARY OF CONGRESS CATALOGING-IN-PUBLICATION DATA

Patchett, Kaye.
  Eli Whitney / Kaye Patchett.
    p. cm. -- (Giants of science)
Summary: Surveys the life and accomplishments of American inventor and mechanic Eli Whitney, who is best known for building the cotton gin, a machine to separate cotton fiber from its sticky seeds.
Includes bibliographical references and index.
  ISBN 1-56711-461-X (hardcover : alk. paper)
  1. Whitney, Eli, 1765-1825. 2. Inventors--United States--Biography.
[1. Whitney, Eli, 1765-1825. 2. Inventors.] I. Title. II. Series.

  TS1570.W4P38 2003
  609.2—dc21

                                                                    2003010684

Printed in China
10 9 8 7 6 5 4 3 2 1

CONTENTS

Bad News

The pitching of the waves became a gentle rocking. The ship had docked at New Haven. Up on deck, the sound of heavy footsteps could be heard as friends boarded to welcome travelers back to Connecticut. Eli Whitney rose from a bunk too short for his tall, sturdy frame and swayed dizzily. Though still weak from the malaria attack that had delayed his business in New York, he was eager to get back to his cotton gin workshop.

Two years before, in 1793, Whitney had invented a machine that could quickly separate cotton fiber from its sticky green seeds. Separating the fiber by hand was a time-consuming and tedious process. This work was usually done by slaves, and it took one person a whole day to produce one pound of cleaned cotton. Using Whitney's cotton gin (short for "engine"), fifty times more cotton could be cleaned in a day. Planters had not previously found it worthwhile to grow cotton because it was

Above: *Slaves cleaned cotton by hand prior to Eli Whitney's invention of the cotton gin.*
Opposite: *Whitney gained national recognition for his cotton gin and many innovations in manufacturing.*

so difficult to process. The cotton gin transformed what used to be a worthless crop into a money-making proposition. Because of the new invention, southern farmers began to plant vast areas of their land with cotton.

Whitney's partner and financial backer, Phineas Miller, lived in the South. When Miller saw how much cotton had been planted, he wrote to Whitney and begged him to make more machines quickly. The shop needed to work fast to produce enough gins to process the huge crop.

On the ship, Whitney grasped the carved wooden rail and climbed up on deck to meet his friends and breathe the crisp March air. He smiled a greeting as he approached briskly and set down his bag. He wanted to tell them of the loan he had just renewed. The new business was short of money in this early stage, but the partners believed that the cotton gin would earn them a fortune.

No one returned his smile. Then one man stepped forward. Awkwardly, he grasped Whitney's hand. Another laid a hand on his shoulder. Whitney looked from one to the other. Finally the first man broke the news. The night before, Whitney's work-shop, with all his tools, materials, and twenty finished cotton gins, had burned to the ground. He was ruined.

A New Nation

In 1783, when Eli Whitney was seventeen, the end of the Revolutionary War had brought hard times to the new nation of the United States of America. The eight-year war had resulted in a disastrous economic slump. The central states still produced cattle and grain for domestic use, but after the war many export markets were lost. The British West Indian ports where America had traded before the Revolution were closed to U.S. ships.

The South was in worse shape. The land was devastated by battles and entire towns had been destroyed. Isolated and impoverished, southern farmers struggled to make a living. Slaves had been killed or taken by the enemy, and once well-tended rice fields had fallen into neglect, never to recover. Tobacco farming exhausted the land, and overproduction had made the crop unprofitable to grow. Cheap indigo from India

George Washington (pictured on white horse) led American troops to victory in the Revolutionary War. After the war, however, the United States experienced economic hard times.

forced indigo farmers out of business. Southern farmers raised potatoes and grain, but much land was uncultivated for the want of a profitable crop.

The country had rich resources of timber, minerals, and farmland, but manpower and machinery were in short supply. Money was scarce. If the nation was to become rich and powerful, it needed labor-saving inventions that could do the work of many people. It also needed an export to form the mainstay of the new economy—something that would be in high demand abroad.

The Right Man at the Right Time

Eli Whitney's cotton gin was the invention that the South had been waiting for. A man named Samuel Slater from England had started a new textile industry in 1789 in Providence, Rhode Island. He had secretly memorized how English inventor Richard Arkwright's mechanical spinning frame was made, then emigrated and copied the machinery to start America's first textile, or cloth, factories. This greatly increased the demand for cotton but, try as they might, farmers could not find a way to process the short-staple, or upland variety, of cotton that grew so easily in the South, and so they were unable to take advantage of this promising new market.

When the cotton gin was invented, an immense and profitable cotton industry arose that rapidly brought wealth to southern planters. The cotton gin reduced labor and caused trade to flourish. It turned cotton into an inexpensive, widely available commodity.

By 1819, just twenty-six years after Whitney invented the cotton gin, the United States produced two-thirds of the world's cotton. Once more expensive than garments made of silk, fine cotton clothing became so cheap that rich and poor alike could wear it. Also, for the first time ever, clothes were easy to wash. Cotton was not only cheaper than wools and silks, it was more hygienic.

Samuel Slater started a U.S. textile industry that greatly increased the demand for cotton.

Supplied with cotton processed by Whitney's cotton gin, Slater's textile mill (pictured) produced inexpensive cotton materials.

Whitney's cotton gin had revolutionized the nation's economy, but he himself was never able to make a profit from it. Eventually, he abandoned his cotton gin business and turned to gun manufacture. His factory was the first to produce interchangeable parts for goods on a large scale. Whitney's gun parts were uniform, or identical in size, and they would fit into any one of the guns he made. Before Whitney invented his system of production each gun was made separately, and its parts would fit only that particular gun. His system of using machines and unskilled workers to make uniform parts was adopted nationwide, as were many of the factory machines that he invented. As the Industrial Revolution gained momentum in America, Whitney's methods were used in the manufacture of everything from clocks to sewing machines. His genius can still be seen in present-day assembly line methods, and in the modern machine tool industry.

A Farm Family in Massachusetts

Eli Whitney was born on December 8, 1765, in Westborough, Massachusetts. He was the eldest child of Eli and Elizabeth Fay Whitney. He had three siblings, Elizabeth, Benjamin, and Josiah. Though not well-to-do, young Eli's father provided for his family and was respected by the little community as one of its most prominent citizens. He held town office and served as a justice of the peace for many years.

Eli's mother became an invalid when Eli was only five years old, after the birth of his youngest brother, Josiah. She was bedridden for most of the next seven and a half years, until her death in 1777. The children were cared for by a housekeeper until their father remarried two years later to Judith Hazeldon, who brought with her two daughters from a previous marriage. A cold woman, she cared little for her stepchildren.

A Young Mechanical Genius

Because of his mother's illness, Eli became self-reliant at an early age. He helped with household chores and assisted his father on the farm. Before school each morning, he had to feed and water sixty cattle. He did his chores dutifully, but much preferred to work in his father's workshop with its pungent smell of metal and wood shavings. In it were a lathe and other tools used to make wheels and furniture and to repair broken farm machinery. Eli quickly learned to handle tools. He delighted in making things and discovering how they worked. When his farm work was done, he could usually be found making something in the workshop.

"He [Eli] was remarkable for thinking and acting for himself at the age of ten or twelve years. . . . I have heard it remarked that at the age of twelve he had more general information than men considered of first standing in the country."

—WHITNEY'S SISTER ELIZABETH, RECALLING HER FAMOUS BROTHER'S CHILDHOOD

When Eli was twelve, his father returned from a few days' absence. He asked what Eli had done while he was gone. The housekeeper told him that Eli had made a violin. Neighbors marveled at how well finished the fiddle was, and said it was exceptional work for a boy to produce. Eli's father was unimpressed. He said his son would never earn a living if he wasted time making something so impractical. When people began to hire Eli to repair violins and other items, he admitted that Eli's hobby was more practical than he had supposed.

Fascinated with how everyday objects were made, young Eli secretly took apart and reassembled his father's watch.

Eli continued to be fascinated by how things were put together. His father's watch was the most complicated mechanism he had ever seen, and he longed to examine it. One Sunday, he pretended to be ill so he could stay home from church. While the family was out, Eli took the watch apart to see how it worked, then put it neatly back together again by the time the churchgoers returned.

Eli's stepmother was annoyed by his habit of investigating how everything was made. Her most prized possession was a set of dinner knives, and when Eli declared that he could make an identical knife, and could even make the tools he would need to make it, she thought he was making fun of her. A short time afterward, one of the knives was broken. True to his word. Eli made another exactly like it. She was pleased, and afterward she stopped scorning Eli when he told her what he could make.

Eli Goes into Business

Eli was nine years old when the shot that started the Revolutionary War in 1775 was fired just thirty miles from the Whitney family farm. As a youngster, Eli watched soldiers marching and heard exciting tales of British raids and American bravery. In school, Eli was slow at learning to read and took little interest in literature, but he surprised his parents and teachers with his outstanding ability in arithmetic. He was fascinated by facts and practical problems.

While on his journey to find an assistant, Eli visited craftsmen's workshops to learn about tools and techniques.

As the war continued, goods became scarce. The price of nails was high. When Eli was fourteen, he persuaded his father to install a forge in the workshop. He made his own tools and went into business making and selling nails in addition to going to school and working on the farm.

After he had been in business for about a year, Eli decided he could make more money if he hired an assistant. He borrowed a horse and set off across the countryside to find a helper. He traveled forty miles in three days, and he visited workshops on the way to learn more about tools and techniques. Craftsmen usually kept their knowledge to themselves, but they did not view the enthusiastic teenage boy as a business rival. They freely showed Eli their methods. Eli's trip proved to be worthwhile. The man he hired stayed for three months and helped the youthful businessman make a profit.

When the war ended, nails became cheap and plentiful. Deprived of a market for his homemade nails, Eli looked for a new opportunity. He noticed that women used long pins to secure their hats. This gave him an idea. Soon he began to manufacture men's walking canes and hatpins for women's bonnets. Meanwhile, the country was struggling economically, and New England farmers were in debt. Like 90 percent of the population, Eli's family made their living from farming. Eli's father would have liked his eldest son to stay home to help on the farm because he was so clever with his hands, but Eli's ambitious nature was dissatisfied, and he sought a way to broaden his opportunities.

Preparation for College

When Eli was nineteen, he decided that he wanted to go to college. His stepmother opposed the idea. Though Eli was even tempered and respectful, his confidence in his own abilities had always irritated her. His father worried about the expense of sending his son to college. Besides, Eli needed more schooling before he could begin a higher education.

Eli resolved to earn his way through school so he could later attend college. He answered an advertisement for a schoolmaster in the neighboring town of Grafton. His father was surprised when Eli was offered the job. Except in arithmetic, his son had not been an especially noteworthy student. Eli studied hard every evening to learn the subjects he had to teach to his pupils. He taught them to cut their own quill pens from a sample he made. Ever the engineer, he believed that well-made tools produced good work.

For three years, Eli attended classes in summer and taught school in winter. He enrolled in Leicester Academy in 1786, where he learned Latin and Greek. There he met Josiah Stebbins, a fellow student who became his lifelong friend.

An Illness and a Turning Point

Toward the end of his time at Leicester Academy, Eli fell seriously ill. He had a fever and an infection, and he lay ill for several weeks. His stepmother and stepsisters soon tired of the extra work of attending to his needs and neglected him. They did not bring his medicine, and they left him alone for hours at a time. Eli's father was angry and made them take better care of him. Annoyed by his wife's uncaring attitude toward his son, he began to show more sympathy for Eli's ambitions. When Eli recovered, his father finally agreed that he could go away to college. No one knows for sure why Eli decided to apply to Yale instead of Harvard College, which was closer, but historians believe that he learned about Yale from Ebenezer Crafts, the principal of Leicester Academy, who was himself a Yale graduate.

Ezra Stiles, the president of Yale College, allowed Whitney to enroll midterm.

A Yale Education

Eli Whitney wanted to improve his higher mathematics skills before taking the Yale entrance examination. He studied with Reverend Elizur Goodrich, a Yale mathematics professor, and formed a close friendship with his son, Elizur Goodrich Jr. Upon Whitney's arrival at Yale in 1789, he was well prepared for the long, arduous test in math, Latin, and Greek. Yale president Ezra Stiles was impressed with Whitney's intelligence and determination. At twenty-three, the tall young man with black hair, a slightly hooked nose, and pleasant features was considerably older than most other students, but he showed a vigorous desire to learn. Convinced of Whitney's abilities, Stiles agreed to admit him midterm so that he could begin his studies without loss of time.

At Yale (pictured), Whitney studied science and developed his social skills. His mechanical aptitude impressed the faculty.

Whitney's classes at Yale reinforced his mechanical genius with a strong foundation of scientific learning. His studies included astronomy, law, chemistry, the art of debate, and the laws of motion. He learned the sciences from Stiles, one of the foremost teachers of science in the country. Whitney was fascinated by the collection of scientific instruments in the college museum. Among these was an orrery, a clockwork device to show how the planets move in the solar system. This device had recently been purchased from England. One day a professor noticed it was out of order. He was about to send it to England for repair, when Whitney asked for permission to try to fix it. Much to the admiration of the faculty, he soon had it working perfectly again.

His time at Yale brought Whitney many friends and taught him to mix easily with people from all levels of society. He found college life stimulating but was constantly worried by a lack of money. Sometimes he colored maps for school friends in return for a little cash. He hoped to earn a good living when he graduated from college, but despite his mechanical genius, he knew of no profession that called for such talents. He decided to study to become a lawyer, though the profession did not interest him particularly. In the meantime, he needed a job. Stiles recommended Whitney for a position as a private tutor for a family in South Carolina. Whitney accepted the job, and graduated from Yale in 1792 at the age of twenty-six. He had his degree at last, but his future seemed as unclear as ever.

Mulberry Grove

Whitney's new job had been arranged by a man named Phineas Miller, who was also a Yale graduate. Miller was the manager of Mulberry Grove, a plantation in Georgia owned by Catherine Greene. He suggested that Whitney travel with him when he sailed from New York to Savannah, Georgia, with Greene and her family after a trip to the North. Greene was the widow of Revolutionary War-hero General Nathanael Greene. She made friends with Whitney during the voyage and invited him to stay at Mulberry Grove for a few days until he was settled in his tutoring position.

When he arrived in the South, Whitney was met with disappointment. The teaching job paid only half what he was promised, and he had to turn it down. He had made the long journey for nothing. When he told Catherine Greene what happened, she invited him to stay at Mulberry Grove and make it his home while he studied to become a lawyer.

An Ingenious Craftsman

Greene was a lighthearted, charming hostess, and Whitney was captivated by her warmth and liveliness. Mulberry Grove was always full of guests; but Whitney's upbringing had accustomed him to working, and he wanted to repay Greene's hospitality. One day as she worked at her embroidery, Greene complained that the frame she used, called a tambour, was clumsily made and tore the threads. Whitney said nothing but went quietly to work. Soon he presented her with a new frame that he had designed himself. She was delighted by its originality and careful craftsmanship. Glad to be useful, he also began to make and repair toys for the Greene children.

Some time later, a group of planters came to visit Mulberry Grove. They were friends of General Greene and had fought

Planters complained that the difficulty of removing seeds from short-staple cotton made it a worthless crop.

under him in the Revolutionary War. The conversation turned to farming, and the planters grumbled and complained about a problem they had discussed countless times before. Upland cotton plants grew as easily as weeds, but they were useless as a crop because there was no efficient way to detach the fiber from its clinging green seeds. In the meantime, thousands of acres of land lay unused, and cotton mills in both America and England were eager to purchase raw cotton. If only someone could invent a machine to separate short-staple cotton, the planters lamented, they would be rich. Then Greene spoke up. "Gentlemen," she said. "Apply to my young friend Mr. Whitney—he can make anything."

A Challenge

When Greene showed the planters her embroidery frame, they were impressed by Whitney's ingenuity. They begged him to try to invent a machine to separate upland cotton. He shook his head modestly and said he had no extraordinary mechanical skills. He said that he had never seen cotton or cotton seed and knew nothing at all about it.

Whitney could never resist a mechanical problem, though. He turned the question over in his mind, then he went to Savannah and searched for some raw cotton. He had to hunt until he was tired, because cotton was out of season, and no one could tell him where some might be found. Finally, in a corner of a dusty warehouse, he discovered a small parcel of cotton on the seed. He bought the parcel and hurried back with it to Mulberry Grove.

Close examination showed Whitney that the cotton bolls consisted of fluffy fibers that stuck tightly to a sticky, velvety

Whitney examined cotton bolls (pictured) and formulated an idea for a machine that could separate the bolls' fibers from the seeds.

green coating on the seeds. It took him only a few days to hit on an idea for a machine to clean the cotton. When he told Phineas Miller, Greene's plantation manager, that he thought he could build the machine after all, Miller was excited. He gave Whitney a basement workshop where he would not be disturbed, and Whitney set to work.

A Different Kind of Cotton

The task before Whitney was a difficult one. Up until that time, the only cotton that could be separated by machine was long-staple, or black-seed cotton. Also known as Sea Island cotton, it grew only in the Caribbean region and on sandy islands off the coast of Georgia. Its smooth black seeds were separated by machines with large rollers. The machines were based on a device called a *charka* that was used in ancient India. These machines pulled the long-staple cotton through a set of rollers like an old-fashioned clothes wringer. Grooves in the rollers caught the lint and pulled it easily from the smooth seeds. If upland cotton was put in the machines, it either went through the rollers along with its seeds, or the seeds were crushed to fragments between the rollers and became mixed with the fiber.

"Do not let a deficiency of money, do not let any thing hinder the speedy construction of the gins. The people of the country are almost running mad for them. . . . When the present crop is harvested, there will be a real property of at least fifty thousand, yes, of a hundred thousand dollars, lying useless, unless we can enable the holders to bring it to market."

— PHINEAS MILLER, FROM A LETTER TO WHITNEY DATED OCTOBER 26, 1794.

Whitney Invents the Cotton Gin

Whitney had never seen the machines for separating long-staple cotton, but he watched carefully to see how slaves separated the green-seed cotton by hand. He saw how they

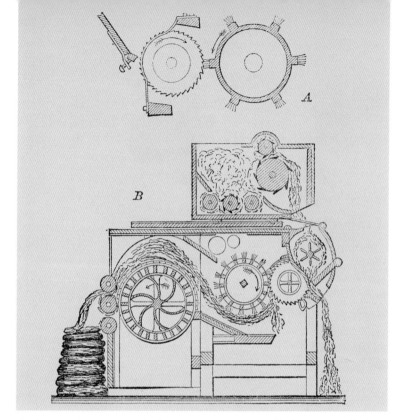

Whitney's design used wires on a rotating cylinder to comb the cotton from the seeds. A second cylinder brushed the cleaned cotton into a hopper.

held the seeds and combed off the fiber, then he set about mechanizing the same process.

A popular legend says that Whitney got the idea for the cotton gin when he saw a cat reach through a wire fence to grab a chicken. When it pulled its paw back through the narrow space in the wires, all it held in its claws was a clump of feathers. Historians do know that Whitney decided to use wires in his machine to pull the cotton fiber off the seeds, much like a cat claws the feathers off a bird.

When Whitney started to make his model cotton gin, he found that the plantation offered only the most basic materials. He had to work with whatever he could find. At first, he thought of using a toothed iron wheel to tear the fiber from the seeds, but there was no suitable sheet iron available. Then he noticed a bundle of iron wire hanging in the parlor. It had been purchased for one of Greene's daughters to make a bird cage.

He decided to use it to make teeth for his invention and carried it down to his workshop.

The model quickly took shape. Whitney attached rows of hooked wire teeth to a wooden cylinder and made a slotted iron guard. When the cylinder was rotated, the teeth reached through the slots in the guard and dragged the fiber from the clinging seeds. The seeds, too large to fit through the slots, fell into a box below. Now Whitney had to think of a way to remove the fiber from the rows of wire hooks. A story tells that Catherine Greene gave him the idea to use rotating brushes, when she suggested jokingly that he should use her fireside brush to clean off the cotton fiber. There is no record of how he really thought of the idea, but he did build a second cylinder, set with bristles, into his model. When he turned the crank handle, the two cylinders turned in opposite directions. As the wire teeth passed through the narrow slots and filled with cotton fiber, the brush swept the cleaned cotton into a hopper designed to collect it. The cotton gin had been invented after only ten days of work.

A New Partnership

It took Whitney another six months of hard work to perfect his machine. The Greene children heard hammer blows and the rasp of a saw through the locked basement door and wondered what their friend was doing. Only Miller and Greene were allowed into the mysterious workshop. By spring of 1793, the machine was as flawless as Whitney could make it.

Miller realized that the basement workshop held an invention that could change the face of southern agriculture forever. He encouraged Whitney to abandon his idea of becoming a lawyer and devote himself instead to establishing a cotton gin business. Whitney was more cautious. He was unwilling to give up the prospect of a well-paid profession for a new enterprise that would be costly to develop. Miller pressed him to change his mind. He offered to pay all of Whitney's expenses in return for a half share in any profits the invention might earn. Whitney consented to try the idea and agreed to go into a partnership with Miller.

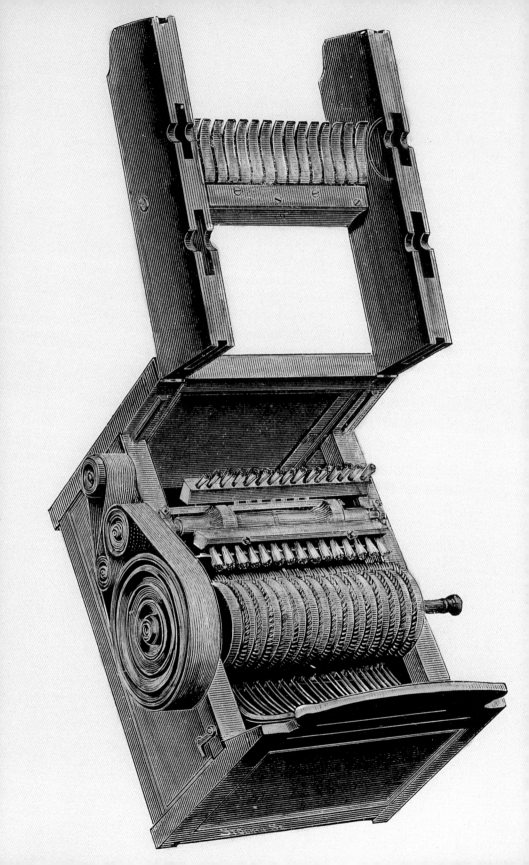

The Secret Becomes Known

Greene had a temporary building erected to house Whitney's invention. Eager to show her friends what Whitney had made, she invited planters from all over Georgia to see the cotton gin. They were astounded when they saw how fast the hopper filled with cleaned cotton as Whitney turned the handle of the polished wooden device. Whitney told them that if the machine was turned by horsepower, it could clean fifty times more cotton in a day than one person could clean by hand.

Friends urged Whitney to get a patent for the cotton gin. He was encouraged by their excitement and believed that his invention would make him rich. He decided to apply for a patent and set up a factory to manufacture cotton gins. In a letter to his father, he wrote, "Tis generally said by those who know anything about it, that I shall make a Fortune by it."

The partners wanted to keep the invention secret from the public until they could obtain a patent. This proved impossible. Soon, people all over the state were talking about the cotton gin. One night, the building where the gin was kept was broken into, and the model was stolen. Before Whitney could apply for a patent, some people had already copied the machine and put their own versions into operation.

Applying for a Patent

The theft of his model startled Whitney into action. If his invention was important enough to steal, he realized that he should establish his rights to it without delay. In June 1793, Whitney traveled to Philadelphia, the nation's capital, and filed his application for a patent. As secretary of state, Thomas Jefferson was the official in charge of receiving patent requests. When Jefferson read the description of the gin, he was intrigued. He asked Whitney if he could buy one to use himself on his own plantation. Whitney was pleased by Jefferson's interest but replied that he had not yet manufactured any full-size machines. Jefferson told Whitney that before the patent could be granted, Whitney must bring a model of the gin, together with detailed designs and drawings, to the patent office.

Opposite: *A finished model of Whitney's cotton gin.*

23

Starting Production

After he had filled out his patent application, Whitney went to New York to buy some equipment for the cotton gin workshop he planned to build in New Haven, Connecticut. He had selected New Haven because materials and skilled workers were more readily available there than in the South. In New York he bought pliers, files, and ninety-six pounds of iron wire. Since he intended to manufacture a large number of cotton gins for the new firm of Miller and Whitney, he realized that he would need more wire to make the teeth. Because it was difficult to make, wire was not manufactured in the United States but had to be imported from France. Whitney's early experience in making nails had taught him how to work with thin lengths of metal, and when he returned to New Haven two weeks later to set up his shop, he bought materials to build his own wire-making equipment.

It took time to get the workshop set up and ready for production. The only tools Whitney could buy were hammers, saws, files, and chisels. He had to make all other tools, even screws, by hand. One component at a time, he constructed a lathe and a turning tool of his own design. The cotton gins he manufactured would be much larger than his first working model. His next tasks were to experiment with ways to make bigger gins and to devise methods to make them as quickly as possible.

Delays

As the summer advanced, Whitney battled new setbacks. An attack of malaria forced him to take to his bed with headaches and fever. A person who had caught malaria, as Whitney had in Georgia, was never fully cured, and the symptoms recurred at intervals. When he recovered, he completed his drawings for the U.S. Patent Office. He believed that his patent would soon be granted, but in August, an outbreak of yellow fever in Philadelphia brought many businesses to a standstill, and Whitney's patent application lay unattended in an untouched pile.

Opposite: *This painting depicts Whitney in his cotton gin workshop in New Haven, Connecticut.*

While he waited impatiently for the patent office to resume business, new difficulties claimed Whitney's attention. The longer rollers that he needed for the large cotton gins proved unexpectedly difficult to make. Every time Whitney drove in the rows of wire teeth, the wood split and splintered under the strain. A month went by as he tried first one kind of wood and then another. Then he had an idea. He noticed that he had driven the wires into the wood parallel with the grain. He made one more wooden cylinder. This time he drove each wire across the grain of the wood. It held firm. He had found the answer. By February 1794, Whitney had made six full-size gins, as well as a small model to deposit at the Patent Office.

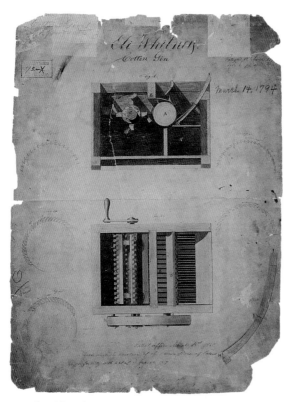

On March 14, 1794, Whitney was granted a patent (pictured) for his cotton gin.

The Patent Is Granted

When Whitney arrived in Philadelphia, he showed his model cotton gin to Edmund Randolph, the new secretary of state. Randolph asked leading government officials to inspect the gin. They marveled at the simple but ingenious device and agreed it was a vital asset to the nation. Randolph granted the patent on March 14, 1794.

Whitney was encouraged by the recognition his cotton gin received in Philadelphia and looked forward to the future.

A patent lasted for fourteen years. It was intended to protect the rights of an inventor to his own invention during that time. Whitney was elated. After sixteen months of work and worry, his claim to the cotton gin appeared to be secure.

While he was in the capital to obtain his patent, Whitney made an influential friend in the government. His old tutor, Elizur Goodrich, had given him a letter of introduction to Oliver Wolcott, the comptroller of the U.S. Treasury and a Yale graduate. Wolcott was particularly interested in new inventions. He welcomed Whitney. He had seen the model gin in action and was eager to hear more about it. Whitney was delighted to receive so much recognition for his invention and traveled back to New Haven with high hopes for the future.

Business Decisions

Soon after Whitney returned to New Haven, he set out on the long journey to Georgia to deliver his finished cotton gins. Before the gin was patented, Phineas Miller had already published an advertisement. It appeared in the *Gazette of the State of Georgia* on March 6, 1794. It announced that Miller and Whitney would gin "any quantity of the green seed cotton" in return for one pound of the cleaned cotton from every five pounds taken to them to be ginned. It promised that gins would be set up all over the country before the next cotton crop was harvested.

Miller and Whitney had decided to lease their own gins rather than sell them. They knew they could not make enough machines to sell individually to every planter. They also realized that the price of one cotton gin, around five hundred dollars, would be too expensive for many farmers. They planned to set up gins at key locations to handle the demand in each area.

An Anxious Time

Miller worked tirelessly to raise loans to finance the new gins. He traveled all over the country to buy sites that had waterpower and to erect ginneries. He hired managers and soon had twenty-five gins operating in different locations across Georgia. Whitney then returned to New Haven to speed the manufacturing process.

When Whitney arrived back at his workshop, bad news awaited him. A ship had brought yellow fever to New Haven, and several of Whitney's workmen had caught the disease. Work had to slow down until the men recovered. Meanwhile, Miller wrote frantic letters to Whitney to remind him of the desperate need for gins to process the immense cotton crop.

Piracy

Whitney understood Miller's urgency. The partners needed to hustle their ginning business into action. In January 1795, the manager of one of Miller's Georgia ginneries reported to Miller that pirated versions of the cotton gin were being operated. Many more copies of the invention were soon in use.

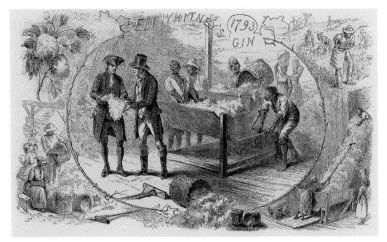

Whitney and his business partner, Phineas Miller, decided to lease Whitney's gins and accept as payment one pound of cleaned cotton for every five pounds brought to them.

The main offenders were Edward Lyon and Hodgen Holmes. Both claimed to have invented improved gins. Holmes's saw gin was just like Whitney's machine, except that it used toothed circular saw blades instead of wires. Whitney had already thought of this idea when he invented the cotton gin, and he had even included it in his patent drawings.

In the midst of doubts and uncertainty, Whitney left New Haven in March 1795 for a business trip to New York. He had to renew a loan to finance his shop. If he could continue to manufacture at a good pace, he believed Miller and Whitney would win out against the people who wanted to infringe on their business enterprise.

Misfortune Strikes

Another attack of illness kept Whitney in New York for three weeks, but at last he boarded the ship back to New Haven. He felt optimistic. Soon he would be back at his workshop. He had twenty cotton gins almost ready to ship and was confident that he could make as many more in a few months. When the ship docked, he was stunned to learn that his shop and everything in it had burned to the ground the day before. As well as the completed gins, his papers and all of the tools he had made were lost.

It was a crushing blow, but Whitney refused to admit defeat. With characteristic energy, he set about the task of rebuilding. Because he had already perfected his manufacturing methods and machine tools, he was able to re-create them quickly. In just seven months, he rebuilt his workshop and made twenty-six more cotton gins. Finances were another matter. Investors had lost confidence after the fire, and it became difficult to borrow money. Whitney struggled with unpaid bills and crushing debts as he fought to keep his shop open.

The Planters Object

Letters from Miller brought more bad news. The planters were angry. They said that Miller and Whitney wanted too much cotton in exchange for their ginning services. They resented Miller and Whitney's attempt to control the ginning business and said that the partners wanted to get rich at their expense. To make matters worse, more cotton had been planted than Miller and Whitney could ever handle. Farmers used this as an excuse to make their own rough copies of the gin to clean their cotton. Too late, the partners realized that instead of trying to do all the ginning themselves, they should have sold the rights to allow people to make their own gins.

Rival gins were everywhere. People ignored Whitney's rights. They even said that Whitney had not really invented the cotton gin. This attack on his good name upset Whitney more than anything else. He felt that his honor was being questioned. Then the planters began to spread a rumor that Miller and Whitney's cotton gins damaged the cotton fiber. English cotton mills believed these untrue reports, and for two years they refused to buy Miller and Whitney's cotton.

The Increase of Slavery

While the new cotton industry rapidly enriched southern planters, the invention of the cotton gin brought only misery for the slaves who labored on the plantations. Before Whitney invented the cotton gin, the slave trade was dying out. Because farming did not pay, the price of slaves had dropped drastically. Planters could not afford their keep. As cotton spread like a

The growth of the southern cotton industry, facilitated by the efficiency of the cotton gin, revitalized the South's economy and required more slaves to pick the now-immense crop.

white ocean across the land, the demand for slaves grew. The cotton gin made processing cotton much easier, but many more slaves were now required to grow and pick the immense crop. For slaves, the cotton gin did not represent progress, as it did for the plantation owners. As the price of land and slaves rose steeply, the new invention increased and reinforced the southern system of slavery.

An Unfair Verdict

The scramble to gain wealth from cotton brought increased conflict. The planters continued to thrust aside the claims of the man who had invented the cotton gin. By the end of 1796, many of Miller and Whitney's thirty ginneries lay idle. The company faced utter ruin. Miller decided his only hope was to sue the people who had copied the cotton gin. In early 1797, the first case, against Edward Lyon, came to trial. The judge

Whitney and Miller lost their lawsuit against planters when a jury ruled that slaves could legally operate pirated copies of Whitney's cotton gin.

showed that he believed Miller and Whitney had right on their side. The jury, meanwhile, was made up of local planters. It would be against their interests to support Miller and Whitney's rights. Their verdict went in favor of Lyon. Miller and Whitney had lost. The jury had used the wording of the patent law to defeat them. The way the law was written in 1793 made it illegal to make and use a patented machine. The copiers of Whitney's invention simply made sure that only slaves used it. As long as people who made a machine did not use it themselves, the law had no power to stop them.

A Turning Point

Whitney was filled with bitterness at the unfair verdict. At almost thirty-two years of age, he felt he had little to show for all of his work and sacrifice. In the fall of 1797, he wrote to Miller: "It is better not to live than to live as I have for three years past. Toil, anxiety and Disappointment have broken me down. My situation makes me perfectly miserable." Miller had married Catherine Greene in 1796. There are no records to show that Whitney and Greene were anything more than good friends, but historians believe that Whitney may have cared for her more deeply and been envious of Miller's marriage to Greene. Whitney told Miller that he would like to marry too, but because of his poor circumstances, he could not "even think of matrimony."

Miller had other business interests, but Whitney had nothing but his own ingenuity to fall back on. While Miller continued to fight in the courts to defend their patent rights, Whitney abandoned the cotton gin business and racked his brain for a new, profitable venture. He analyzed the reasons for Miller and Whitney's failure. One of their biggest problems had been finding enough money. Raising loans for a new enterprise would be even more difficult. After much thought, he had an inspiration. The government had funds to purchase goods for the nation, and Whitney was already known for his mechanical abilities. If he could get a government contract, he would not have to worry about how to raise money. What could he offer to make for the government?

A Government Contract

Whitney's opportunity came early in 1798. War between the United States and France seemed likely, and guns were in short supply. Most weapons for the Revolutionary War had been purchased from France, but this was now impossible. The federal government did not have enough time or manpower to make the thousands of guns it needed. Advertisements were printed seeking private contractors who could make muskets. Whitney wrote to Oliver Wolcott at the Treasury Department and offered his services. He explained that he already had machinery and trained workmen. He said he was confident that he could easily adapt his techniques to make musket parts quickly and efficiently by machine.

In 1798 Whitney agreed to make muskets for the U.S. government. The resulting contract saved the inventor from financial ruin.

The government's armory at Springfield, Massachusetts, had made one thousand stands of arms during the last three years (a stand of arms included a musket, a bayonet, and a ramrod). Whitney proposed to make ten or fifteen thousand. To make so many muskets, Whitney would need to use methods that the nation had never seen before. From anyone else, the idea would have sounded impossible, but Wolcott knew and

This engraving shows Whitney's new arms factory next to the Mill River. Whitney and his crew built the factory during Connecticut's harsh winter months.

admired Whitney's genius. Within three and a half weeks, a contract was signed between Eli Whitney and the U.S. government for delivery of ten thousand stands of arms by September 30, 1800. Whitney wrote to tell his old friend Josiah Stebbins about his good fortune: "By this contract I obtained some thousands of Dollars in advance which has saved me from ruin." Now Whitney could pay his debts and start afresh.

The Arms Factory

It was a daring project. Whitney had no buildings suitable for an arms factory, and he had yet to hire more workmen and design all the tools he would need to make musket parts. Until he made his proposal to the government, he had never even examined how a musket was made. He bought a mill site at Mill Rock in the town of Hamden, just north of New Haven. The site was next to Mill River and had a waterfall to supply waterpower to turn his machinery. Whitney and a crew of workmen toiled in the snows of a harsh winter to build the factory and a dam. Often their fingers were so cold, they could hardly hold the heavy tools or fit one brick on top of another. They squelched and crunched through mud and ice. Many times it snowed so hard that they had to wait for the storm to

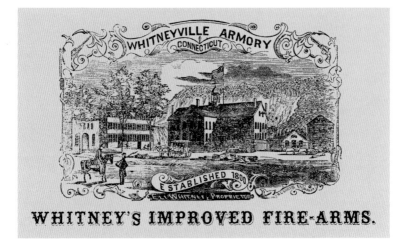

WHITNEY'S IMPROVED FIRE-ARMS.

Whitney looked after the workers at his armory, depicted in this advertisement, in many ways. He built the United States's first mill town, Whitneyville, to house his employees.

pass before they could carry on. At last, on January 12, 1799, Whitney wrote to Stebbins, "My building which is 72 feet long by 30 and 2 stories high is nearly finished!"

Whitney paid attention to every detail of his new operation. He knew that his workforce was just as important as the factory itself. He did not want to lose good workers once he had trained them. He reasoned that family men would be less likely to move on if they were well housed and cared for. Beneath a sheltering wooded hillside, he built a row of workers' houses and a large boardinghouse for unmarried men. The site, which became known as "Whitneyville," was the first mill village to be built in the United States. Whitney was more than just an employer. He helped his workers when they were sick, and he acted like a kindly but strict father to the many apprentices— boys who were sent by their parents to his factory to learn a trade in the manufacturing industry.

Interchangeable Parts

Whitney's arms factory changed the way that guns and other complex mechanisms were manufactured in the United States. Muskets were traditionally made by skilled craftsmen, who shaped every part by hand. Each musket had about fifty different parts. The most intricate part of a musket was the lock, or firing mechanism. Because the parts were handmade, it was impossible to make each one the same size. This meant that if a musket was damaged, a new part had to be handcrafted to fit that particular gun.

Whitney had to make a lot of guns in a short time, so he had to use different methods. In his factory, he broke down the work of making muskets into many individual steps. He designed specialized machinery for each task. The parts Whitney made for his musket locks were all the same size and would fit together interchangeably. This process, called division of labor, meant that even an inexperienced workman could quickly learn one or a few steps in any manufacturing process. Because in Whitney's factory machines were specially designed to make parts of a certain size, accuracy depended on machines, not craftsmen.

Other Inventors

Eli Whitney was the first person in the country to use factory mass production on a large scale, but he did not claim to have invented the idea of interchangeable parts. In Europe, in 1788, a Frenchman named Honorá Blanc invented a way to make musket parts using machinery. Unlike Whitney, who made only the locks with identical parts, Blanc made other parts of the musket to be interchangeable, including the barrel and stock. Thomas Jefferson saw and admired Blanc's work during a visit to France and tried without success to persuade him to move to the United States. Because France had many skilled craftsmen who could make weapons by hand, Blanc's method was not widely used and disappeared after his death.

In England, too, people worked to substitute machines for skilled labor. In 1793 Sir Samuel Bentham and Marc Brunel invented machinery to make wooden pulley blocks for the Royal Navy. In the rigging of their ships, the navy used more than a hundred thousand of the blocks a year, all of which had to be handmade. Bentham's and Brunel's machines allowed 10 unskilled workers to do the work of 130 craftsmen.

In the United States, most inventors worked in isolation. Bad roads, few newspapers, and a slow postal system made communication difficult, even between towns just a dozen or so miles apart. In 1799 a man named Simeon North had a workshop only twenty miles from Whitney. In the early 1800s North also designed and used machines to make pistols with interchangeable parts, yet historians believe that he and Whitney never met.

More Delays

Because Whitney had to invent every stage of his new musket-making process for himself, it took time to get his factory ready to start. The cruel winter that had turned construction into a battle had also made it impossible to dig iron ore, and deliveries of raw materials were slow. Whitney became frustrated. When he promised to have ten thousand muskets finished in two years, he did not realize how much time he would need to get set up. He could have hurried his factory into production, but he knew that would only result in poor quality work. Eli Whitney was a perfectionist. He knew he could make better muskets than anyone in the country, but he had to convince the authorities to give him more time.

There had been changes in the government since Whitney signed his arms contract. Wolcott was no longer in the Treasury Department, and Thomas Jefferson had been elected president. Whitney had new officials to deal with—people who knew nothing of his innovative methods. Although he had already made piles of various musket parts, he had yet to perfect some of the machine tools he needed to make others. The fall of 1800 passed and he had no finished muskets to send. Somehow, he had to explain to the War Department why he had not yet fulfilled his contract and convince them that his muskets were worth waiting for.

The Demonstration

In January 1801 Whitney met with outgoing president John Adams and other dignitaries in Washington, the new capital. The group of blue-coated men, which included Whitney's old

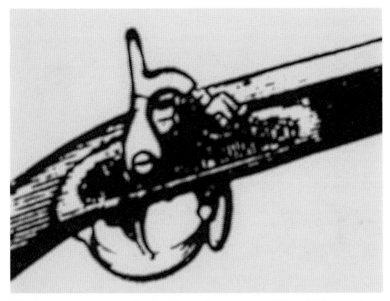

Whitney's demonstration of the interchangeability of his musket-lock parts impressed President John Adams and other officials.

friend Elizur Goodrich Jr., now a U.S. congressman, watched curiously as Whitney, well dressed and self-assured, set a large box on the polished wooden table in front of them. Thomas Jefferson leaned forward in his seat to see what Whitney had brought. Whitney reached into the box, and soon the tabletop was covered with small piles of metal parts. Deftly, he took one part at random from each pile, and before the men's astonished gaze, he quickly assembled a complete musket lock. He invited the fascinated officials to try for themselves. Intrigued, everyone present reached forward and picked out a handful of the smooth, oddly shaped pieces of metal. As they assembled locks and then took them apart and tried different components, they exclaimed in wonder. Every time, the parts fitted together smoothly and exactly. Whitney's hands-on demonstration had convinced them. Jefferson said that he had seen no work in the nation equal to Whitney's.

Whitney returned to New Haven with the promise of five more years to complete his contract, and an additional twenty

Because of his bad experience with the cotton gin patent, Whitney refused to submit any of his new inventions to the U.S. patent office (pictured).

thousand dollars in advance payments. The government was in less of a hurry for new weapons than it had been at the start of Whitney's contract. Relations with France had improved, and war now seemed unlikely. Delighted by his success and relieved of the need for haste, Whitney went to work to perfect his machine tools and his factory system.

No More Patents

After his visit to Washington, Whitney's reputation soared. The government, as well as private arms contractors, began to ask his advice about making guns. Whitney's musket factory ran smoothly, and on September 26, 1801, he had five hundred stands of arms finished and ready for delivery. In a letter to Samuel Dexter, the new secretary of the treasury, he wrote: "My system I now consider as established and my theory successfully reduced to practice."

One of the most important early devices used in Whitney's factory was a filing jig. It used clamps, or molds, to hold a piece of work firmly in place. A workman would file around the outlines of the mold to make a new part of the same shape. Unlike many tasks in the factory, the filing jig required a skilled workman, because handwork and judgment were needed to file carefully around the mold. Whitney supervised closely to make sure that every mold was made properly. All day long, he hurried from one workroom to another to shout directions over the roar and clatter of power-driven machinery.

There are no records of all the machines Whitney invented for his factory. He refused to patent any more inventions. When his friends told him that he needed to protect his rights, he pointed out that a patent had not protected his rights to the cotton gin. He had decided that patents only caused trouble.

The Fight for Patent Rights

While Whitney threw his heart and genius into his new arms business, Phineas Miller stubbornly kept up the fight for patent rights to the cotton gin. In 1799 Miller had changed his policy and offered to sell people the right to make their own cotton gins. In the fall of 1801 he wrote to Whitney and begged him to travel south. The state of South Carolina wanted to buy the rights to use the invention. Whitney had just made his first delivery of muskets. He did not want to leave his arms factory, but this was important. He made the long, exhausting journey, and in February 1802, the South Carolina legislature voted to pay Miller and Whitney fifty thousand dollars in three separate payments for rights to use the cotton gin.

Long and bitter struggles were still to come. In 1803 the South Carolina legislature listened to renewed rumors that Whitney had not really invented the saw gin, and demanded back the twenty thousand dollars they had already paid. Angered by this unexpected turn of events, Whitney journeyed south yet again. To his great sorrow, he arrived to learn that Miller had died of a fever on December 7, 1803, at the age of thirty-nine.

Miller's death came when success was almost in sight. The following year, the state of South Carolina restored their

At the turn of the century, Whitney renewed lawsuits against the Georgia planters who used and profited from copies of his cotton gin.

agreement and paid Whitney the rest of the sum they had promised. In the meantime, North Carolina and Tennessee also bought patent rights to the cotton gin.

The End of the Cotton Gin Battles

With money from the sale of patent rights, Whitney could afford to continue the many lawsuits his partner had started. Between 1798 and 1806, the firm of Miller and Whitney brought sixty unsuccessful lawsuits in the state of Georgia against people who had copied the cotton gin. In 1800 the wording of the law that lost them their first case was changed. Now the law made it illegal either to make or use another person's invention without permission. Although other states had admitted Whitney's right to the gin, Georgia planters were still obstinate. Victory came at last in May and December 1806, when two verdicts went in favor of Whitney. In the second case, against Arthur Fort, Judge William Johnson ruled that Hodgen Holmes's saw gin, which Fort had operated, was adapted from Whitney's invention. The judge pointed out that the only difference between the two gins was that Whitney's gin used wire teeth instead of toothed iron plates. Otherwise, Johnson said decisively, "every characteristic of Mr. Whitney's invention is preserved." Whitney was awarded two thousand dollars. He had won back his good name and the rights to his own invention, but overall Whitney saw the thirteen-year venture as a failure. He had spent far more in legal expenses than he ever regained. In 1807 the cotton gin patent expired, and Whitney was not able to renew it.

> "Many Citizens of Georgia are amassing fortunes, living voluptuously and rolling in splendor by the surreptitious use of the gin."
>
> —ELI WHITNEY, COMMENTING BITTERLY ON THE GEORGIANS WHO PIRATED HIS INVENTION.

The Musket Contract Fulfilled

Whitney's many journeys to the South created delays that he could not afford. His arms factory did not run as well if he was not there to supervise things in person, and although he had been able to deliver several batches of finished muskets, he was forced to ask the government to extend his contract several more times. The secretary of war, Henry Dearborn, was impressed by the quality of the muskets that Whitney had already made, and gladly gave him more time.

The boxes that Whitney had used to deliver the muskets were also his invention. He had noticed with disapproval that the boxes usually used to pack guns were not moisture proof. In the past, weapons had often rusted before they were even unpacked. Whitney would have nothing to do with such poor workmanship. He made strong, watertight chests out of seasoned pinewood. In a letter to Dearborn he explained, "I have spared no pains to compleat my Musketts in the best manner.

Whitney packed his firearms in watertight pinewood chests to ensure that they arrived to buyers in perfect condition.

I feel unwilling that they should be spoiled by being improperly packed."

Dearborn valued Whitney's careful work and honesty. In 1807 he offered Whitney a job as head of the national armory at Harpers Ferry, West Virginia, but Whitney refused the offer. In January 1809 Whitney finally completed his government musket contract. It had taken ten years, but he had proved himself as the best musket maker in the country.

Threat of Closure

The muskets that Whitney manufactured were made from a design that the government had given him to copy. Some people have asked why Whitney, with his genius, did not design a musket of his own. His reasons were logical and businesslike. To manufacture a different musket, he would have needed to make a lot of new tools and machines. He could not afford the delays and expense that such a lengthy process would demand. He had designed all of his machinery especially to meet orders from the U.S. government.

With his factory geared to make muskets for the nation, Whitney was thunderstruck to learn, in 1808, that the government did not want him to make any more guns after his contract was finished. The two national armories at Harpers Ferry and Springfield would make all that were needed. Whitney had some tough choices to make. His workmen depended on him for their living. They had raised families in the houses he had built for them in Whitneyville. It would be hard for them to move—and there were no similar jobs for them to go to. Whitney by now had enough money himself to live comfortably, but he had put his whole heart and soul into his factory. He could not give it up now.

Uncertain Times
While Whitney cast around frantically for a way to save his factory, Oliver Wolcott stepped in. No longer a government official, Wolcott lived in New York, where he knew many influential people. The federal government had recently told the states that they must arm their own militias, and Wolcott

The quality of Whitney's muskets earned him a job offer as head of the national armory at Harpers Ferry (pictured), Virginia.

arranged a contract for Whitney with the governor of New York to make two thousand muskets for the New York militia.

Other state contracts followed, which provided enough work to keep Whitney's factory going. In 1812 the United States declared war on Great Britain. The British held Canada and were threatening the westernmost parts of the United States. Whitney at once wrote to Dearborn. The nation would need many more muskets and, he reminded the secretary of war, his was the only factory in the country able to produce them in large numbers. Within three weeks he received a new contract to make fifteen thousand muskets by 1820. The worries and uncertainty of the last four years were over. His factory was saved.

More Threats

For about a year, Whitney's troubles seemed to be behind him. When British blockades made it difficult to get supplies, Whitney's deliveries of muskets had fallen behind schedule, but he was not worried. The government had always been understanding in the past. He did not know that trouble was brewing.

Captain Callendar Irvine, the new commissary general of purchases, was jealous of Whitney. He and a man named Marine Wickham, who also worked for the War Department, had designed a musket of their own. They wanted the government to make their musket at the federal armories and stop buying from Whitney. Irvine tried to change the government's arms-buying policy. He said they should not buy guns from private companies. He did everything in his power to take away Whitney's contract. First, he complained that Whitney's deliveries of muskets were late. Then he told General John Armstrong, the secretary of war, that Whitney's muskets were defective. He said the bayonets were too short, the barrels crooked, and the hammers too sharp. Whitney hotly defended his work. He pointed out that his muskets were made exactly to the design that the government had ordered. Whitney's argument won the day, but he was worried. He knew that if Irvine canceled his government contract, he would be forced to close his factory.

Callendar Irvine and Marine Wickham, who had developed their own musket, tried to convince Secretary of War John Armstrong (pictured) that Whitney's muskets were defective.

Irvine plotted his next move. He wanted to convince the War Department that Whitney's muskets were faulty. Government inspectors always fired a certain number of newly made weapons to check that they were strong enough. This gave Irvine the idea he was looking for. He decided to send Wickham to Whitney's factory to carry out a weapons inspection. When Wickham and his assistant arrived at the Mill Rock

SHAPING THE BARREL.

ROLLING THE BARREL.

FINISHING.

TESTING THE BAYONETS.

POLISHING MACHINE.

STRAIGHTENING THE BARRELS.

POLISHING BAYONETS.

TURNING THE STOCK.

PLANING MACHINE.

PUTTING THE MUSKET TOGETHER.

BORING MACHINE.

RIFLING MACHINE.

MANUFACTURING MUSKETS, U.S. ARMORY, SPRINGFIELD, MASS.

factory, they told Whitney that they had brought gunpowder "of approved strength" to test his muskets. Whitney asked how strong the powder was. When they avoided his question, Whitney bristled with suspicion. He was sure that the men would purposely use enough powder to blow his guns to bits. After four days of furious argument, Whitney refused to allow the tests and turned the inspectors out of his factory.

In February 1815 a peace treaty was signed at Ghent, Belgium, and the war between the United States and Great Britain ended. A new law put a different department in charge of new government musket contracts. This took away some of Irvine's power, but Whitney knew the change might be too late to save his business. His own contract was still in the hands of Irvine, his old enemy. After much thought, Whitney reached for his quill. He wrote a letter directly to President James Madison and explained his plight. The president listened. He transferred inspections to the newly created Ordnance Department, and James Carrington, a man whom Whitney knew and trusted, became the official inspector.

Domestic Affairs

The past seven years had been a time of stress and anxiety for Whitney. Beset by business worries and Irvine's hostility, he had worked himself to exhaustion. In 1810 he had been seriously ill. Many diseases were not recognized in the early nineteenth century, but experts now believe that Whitney suffered from ulcers caused by overwork and stress. For years, he had worked day and night to design improvements to his system, keep his machines in good repair, and to attend to the multitude of tasks that the factory demanded of him.

Whitney had little or no home life. Twelve or more apprentices lived with him in a farmhouse on his property. He hired a housekeeper to cook, wash, clean house, and mend clothes. The work was hard, and housekeepers rarely stayed long.

Opposite: *This nineteenth-century illustration shows the many steps required for manufacturing muskets. The demands of Whitney's work may have contributed to his health problems.*

Whitney also had taken his sister Elizabeth's three sons, Philos, Elihu, and Eli Whitney Blake, to live with him. He had them educated, and he trained them in his own trade. He hoped that one day his nephews would carry on his business. He was fond of children, but rarely had time to be with the three boys; business problems demanded all his attention. He was lonely and longed for a home and family of his own. He described himself in a letter to his friend Stebbins as "an Old Bachelor, overwhelmed in business . . . constantly resolved to marry without allowing myself leasure to take one step towards carrying that resolution into effect."

The Arms Business Flourishes

After the war ended, Whitney heard news that cheered him considerably. Roswell Lee, a former employee at the Mill Rock factory, had been hired to head the national armory at Springfield. At last Whitney had someone with whom he could share some of his business cares. The two men worked closely together. They consulted about workmen's salaries and the best places to buy raw materials and supplies. Whitney also shared with Lee the designs of factory machines that he had invented. As a businessman, Whitney saw his inventions simply as solutions to manufacturing problems. If Lee could use them to make the Springfield armory more efficient, he was welcome.

Freed from the worry of losing his government musket orders, Whitney now had time to improve his machinery. He invented a way to make trip-hammers, used to weld musket barrels, more effective. He passed the idea on to Lee, and also offered him a design for a barrel-turning device that he had invented several years before. Whitney had not bothered to make the machine for himself. If he had made it, he told Lee, some other gun maker would probably "not only take advantage of my invention but intice away the workmen whom I had instructed in the use of the Machine before I could be half compensated for the expence of making it." Whitney had learned to be cautious. He trusted Lee, but he knew that dishonest people would always be ready to benefit from his inventions at his own expense.

The President Pays a Visit

Whitney was now at the height of his career. The chief of the U.S. Ordnance Department consulted with him regularly about musket designs and standards for the nation. Hundreds of visitors toured the factory at Mill Rock to listen with close attention as Whitney explained his ingenious system of machinery. He was not afraid that any of his visitors would copy his system to create a similar factory. It was far too complicated for another person to duplicate unless they had drawings and specifications for every single detail.

In 1816 President James Monroe visited the factory during a trip to the eastern states. Whitney shook Monroe's hand warmly and asked what he would like to see. Monroe was interested in every-thing Whitney could show him. He watched how the workers operated the huge, whirring

President James Monroe (pictured) visited Whitney's factory in 1816 and was impressed by the inventor and his inventions.

power-driven machines that turned metal into musket parts. As Whitney demonstrated how this or that device worked, Monroe marveled at his knowledge and enthusiasm. Next, Whitney took Monroe to the huge barn that housed horses, cattle, and farm machinery. The inventor's passion for improvements could be seen everywhere. Whitney pointed out ingenious door fastenings of his own invention. Even the cattle and horses that swished their tails contentedly in their tidy stalls were not forgotten. Whitney had invented a device to keep their halter ropes from getting entangled. Each rope ran through a metal loop. At the end, a small weight stopped the rope from getting entangled. This device allowed the animals to move their heads freely. A tour of Whitney's shops and buildings showed that careful thought had also gone into their construction. Some were made using attractive local stone from the slopes of East Rock. In others, Whitney had used an unusual cement composed partly of sand that he had made by grinding gun barrels and other iron for added strength. Monroe left with no doubt that Whitney's favorite saying was true of all that Whitney undertook: "There is nothing worth doing that is not worth doing well."

A Family at Last

For twenty-three exhausting years, Whitney had devoted himself to his career. Finally, on January 6, 1817, he married Henrietta F. Edwards, the daughter of an old friend, Pierpont Edwards. Whitney was fifty-two; his bride was thirty-one. They had known each other since Henrietta was a child. It is widely believed by historians that Whitney was too attached to Catherine Greene to marry anyone else until after her death in 1814.

Whitney's marriage was a very happy one. The couple had four children. Their eldest child, a daughter, Frances Edwards, was born in November 1817. She was followed by Elizabeth Fay in 1819 and a son, Eli Jr., in January 1821. To the couple's great sorrow, their youngest daughter, Susan Edwards, died when she was twenty-one months old. Whitney had always loved children. He still worked as hard as ever, but he played with his children and was always ready to tell stories about the little things they did. When his brother Josiah sent picture books for the children, Whitney wrote to tell him that "Eli could not consent to go to bed without taking his [book] into bed with him."

The Milling Machine

About a year after his marriage, Whitney developed a mechanized metal-cutting device that was a major leap forward in technology. As with all of his later inventions, he made the milling machine to fill a need in his factory, not to patent it or to sell for profit. The slowest part of his system had always been the filing jig. Although it was vital to his system, the filing jig had a drawback. Only a skilled workman could use it, and the process of filing around a mold to make an irregular-shaped part took so long that the rest of the musket-making process was held up. Whitney needed a machine that was easier to use and could cut parts automatically. The milling machine that he invented in 1818 solved his problem and soon became standard equipment in machine shops across the nation.

> "One of my primary objects is to form the tools so the tools themselves shall fashion the work and give to every part its just proportion—which when once accomplished, will give expedition, uniformity, and exactness to the whole."
>
> —ELI WHITNEY, EXPLAINING HIS FACTORY SYSTEM IN A LETTER TO OLIVER WOLCOTT.

To shape a part with the milling machine, a workman clamped a metal plate to a table on the machine. On top, he clamped the pattern, or template, that he wanted to copy. An iron wheel with sharpened, curved teeth then rotated to follow the shape of the template. Each tooth acted as a separate chisel. A power-driven screw made the wheel rotate, and the teeth automatically chipped away the metal one tiny piece at a time to form an exact copy of the original part.

Simeon North is said to have made a milling machine several years before Whitney had the idea. Because North did not show his machine to many people, it was not generally known and had no impact on the advance of machine tools in the nation's factories. After Whitney invented his milling machine, he at once gave the design to Roswell Lee, and it was soon used as standard equipment in both federal armories.

Another inventor, Thomas Blanchard, invented a machine for making gun stocks at about the same time that Whitney developed the milling machine. The gun stock lathe became known as the Blanchard lathe, but because of Whitney's refusal to patent his own inventions, his name was soon forgotten in association with the widespread use of the milling machine.

A Successful Man

By 1820, Whitney was recognized as the most famous industrialist in the country. People who knew his skill as an engineer asked him to make special equipment for them. In the fall of 1820 he made a complex chemical apparatus for Professor Benjamin Silliman of Yale. Now a wealthy man, Whitney was still dedicated to his life's work. In August 1822 he traveled to Washington and signed a new contract with the government to make fifteen thousand muskets.

When Whitney returned to his family after his journey to the capital, he looked pale and ill. He had been in poor health for the last two years after a bad case of influenza, but this was clearly something more serious. Alarmed, Henrietta sent for the doctor. For three weeks Whitney lay in bed, racked with pain. He was never again completely well. He had an enlarged prostate, and there was no cure.

Whitney's renown as an engineer reached Yale professor Benjamin Silliman (pictured), who asked Whitney to make a complicated chemical apparatus.

Illness

Whitney's doctor was one of the best physicians in the country. When he told Whitney sadly that he was unable to help him, Whitney remained calm. He researched his disease in minute detail and invented instruments to relieve his pain. Professor Silliman said admiringly that Whitney acted "rather as if he himself had been the physician than the patient."

While he was ill, Whitney liked to have his children around him. Sometimes, the younger children opened the drawers and pulled out the contents of their father's bureau for fun. It is thought that their play gave Whitney the idea for another ingenious mechanism. When he felt a little better, Whitney invented a way to lock all the bureau drawers with one turn of a key. Like so many of his inventions, he made it simply for his own convenience, but the device was widely admired and eventually passed into general use. At the end of 1823, Whitney felt improved enough to go about his normal activities again. He knew that his illness would return, and he wanted to make the most of the time that was left to him.

Last Inventions

While his nephew Eli Blake helped to run the factory, Whitney worked feverishly to make improvements to his site. Once again, his tall figure was seen around the buildings and roads in Whitneyville. His stride was less brisk than it had been, and he sometimes had to lean his arm on a workman's sturdy shoulder for support. He inspected the sheds where he stored fuel for the factory. He mused that there must be an easier way to refill the large bins with coal. He glanced up at the hillside that loomed above the storage sheds. He had found the solution. Under Whitney's direction, a road was cut into the rocky slope so that supply wagons could drive above the sheds and tip their loads directly into the bins below.

While he worked to improve his site, Whitney pondered over another problem. He wanted to find a way to smooth down metal parts without having to file and grind them. In August 1824 he wrote to Lee to tell him about a new device he had invented. He sent Lee a drawing of his invention, which was called a tumbler mill. Parts that needed to be smoothed could be placed inside a barrel filled with sand and oil. As the barrel tilted and rotated, the parts would knock together. The friction caused by this process would smooth off the rough edges of the metal. Whitney was excited by his idea. He wrote to Lee, "If it answers my expectations it will form a new era in the business of forging Iron & Steel." He told Lee that he hoped he would be well enough to test the machine himself; but it was not to be. By November his disease once more gripped him in spells of dreadful pain, and his family and friends knew that the end was near.

"His Country Honors His Memory"

Whitney also knew he did not have long to live. He made his will and took care that Henrietta and the children would be well provided for, but he worried constantly about what would become of his factory after he was gone. Although he was in terrible pain, he took much pleasure in seeing his friends. His voice, faint and tired, was still cheerful and courteous. No matter how ill he felt, he was always shaved, and he dressed in neat, clean clothes whenever he had a visitor. Soon his sufferings were so bad that it seemed he must die at any moment. Still, he was tormented by the question of how his unfinished musket contract could be completed. On January 7, 1825, the day before he died, he found the answer. He added a new section to his will, in which he asked his nephews, Eli and Philos Blake, to manage his business until the last musket was made. The next day, he died in peace.

When Whitney's affairs were sorted out, it was discovered that he had been generous with his fortune. His papers showed that he had lent out the huge total of seventy thousand dollars over the years, much of it to young people who wanted to start out in business. The New Haven community mourned their loss. Whitney's kindness and generosity had made him a much loved figure, just as his genius had earned him national respect. His funeral was attended by a large gathering of friends and admirers. The inscription on his tomb reads:

Eli Whitney earned a reputation for generosity in his community and gained national recognition for his genius.

ELI WHITNEY. The inventor of the Cotton Gin. Of useful Science and Arts, the efficient Patron and Improver. In the social relations of life, a Model of excellence. While private affection weeps at his tomb, his country honors his memory.

Whitney's Legacy

Eli Whitney was one of many inventors during the American Industrial Revolution who worked to develop machine tools, but Whitney introduced new techniques and machines that created a fast track for other manufacturers to follow. He did not invent the uniformity system, but he launched it further and faster than any other person of his day. Today he is acknowledged as the father of mass production. Whitney developed a system of division of labor that made up for the country's lack of skilled manpower and set the stage for the United States to become a forceful economic power.

Whitney's invention of the cotton gin caused a surge in the economy of the South that made exports skyrocket. Some forty years after his death, the two dynamic powers that Whitney did so much to create—the wealthy cotton interests of the South and the industrial power of the North—were to meet in bitter battle when the factories of the North made the arms that defeated the South and ended slavery in the American Civil War (1861–1865).

In 1861 arms produced in the North as a result of Whitney's inventiveness threatened the wealth and way of life that his cotton gin brought to the South.

IMPORTANT DATES

1765	Eli Whitney is born on December 8 in Westborough, Massachusetts.
1775	The Revolutionary War begins.
1777	Whitney's mother, Elizabeth Fay, dies. His father remarries two years later, to Judith Hazeldon.
1780	Whitney starts his first business; he makes and sells nails in his father's workshop.
1783	The Revolutionary War ends.
1786	Whitney enrolls in Leicester Academy, where he studies Latin and Greek.
1788	In France, Honorá Blanc mass produces guns with interchangeable parts.
1789	Whitney enters Yale college. Samuel Slater starts the American textile industry in Providence, Rhode Island; there is a high demand for cotton.
1792	Whitney graduates from Yale; he obtains a tutoring job in the South that falls through; he remains in Georgia as a guest of Catherine Greene at her plantation, Mulberry Grove.
1793	Whitney invents the cotton gin; he goes into partnership with Phineas Miller and sets up a workshop at New Haven, Connecticut, to manufacture gins.
1794	Whitney is granted a patent for the cotton gin.
1795	Pirated copies of the gin start to appear; the cotton gin workshop burns down; it is rebuilt seven months later and resumes production.
1796	Miller and Whitney have thirty cotton gins at eight Georgia locations. Planters pirate the gin and spread lies about the quality of Miller's and Whitney's cotton.
1797	The verdict in the first patent infringement trial, against Edward Lyon, goes against Miller and Whitney.
1798	Whitney receives a contract from the U.S. government to make ten thousand muskets.

60

1798–1806	Miller and Whitney bring sixty unsuccessful lawsuits in the state of Georgia over infringements on the cotton gin patent.
1799	Whitney finishes building his musket factory at Mill Rock in the town of Hamden, near New Haven.
1801	Whitney gives a demonstration of interchangeable parts to government officials in Washington, D.C.
1802–1804	South Carolina, North Carolina, and Tennessee buy patent rights to the cotton gin.
1803	Phineas Miller dies of a fever on December 7 at age thirty-nine.
1806	In May and December, Miller and Whitney win their first two patent infringement cases; Judge William Johnson rules that the pirated gins are based on Whitney's invention.
1807	The cotton gin patent expires; Whitney is unable to renew it; he views the cotton gin venture as a failure.
1809	Whitney completes his first government musket contract after ten years.
1812	The United States declares war on Great Britain; Whitney receives a second contract from the government to make fifteen thousand muskets.
1814	Catherine Greene dies.
1816	President James Monroe visits Whitney's arms factory.
1817	Whitney marries Henrietta F. Edwards on January 6; they have four children in the next five years.
1818	Whitney invents the milling machine.
1822	Whitney signs his third government musket contract. He becomes terminally ill shortly afterward.
1823	Whitney temporarily recovers and makes improvements to his site.
1824	Whitney designs the tumbler mill, his last invention.
1825	After a long illness, Eli Whitney dies on January 8 at age fifty-nine.

GLOSSARY

armory: A workshop where armor or weapons are made. The same term is used to refer to a place where weapons are stored.

black-seed cotton: Also known as Sea Island, or long-staple cotton, this variety can only be grown in sandy areas along the coast. Its fiber is easy to separate from its seeds, unlike that of the green-seed, or short-staple cotton that grows readily in the South.

cotton boll: The fruit of the cotton plant. When the oval-shaped fruit ripens, it bursts to reveal a white, fluffy mass of cotton fibers, or lint, which surrounds a large number of seeds.

division of labor: A method used to simplify complex tasks. A complicated process is broken down into a series of simple steps, and a separate worker is assigned to each task. In this way, goods are mass-produced quickly and cheaply, because each worker has to learn only one small, relatively simple job.

hopper: A funnel-shaped bin used to collect the cleaned cotton fiber during the ginning process.

Industrial Revolution: The change from an economy in which goods were made by hand to one in which they were made by factories and machines. The Industrial Revolution began in Europe in the eighteenth century and quickly moved to America. Between 1815 and 1860, large factories and power-driven machinery took the place of the skilled craftsmen and cottage industries of colonial days.

interchangeability/interchangeable parts: A way to manufacture an intricate mechanism so that each of its parts is made to a standard size. The interchangeable parts system became known as "the American System," because it was first widely used in the United States.

lathe: A machine used to shape the surface of a piece of wood or metal. The piece to be shaped is held firmly and rotated against a cutting tool.

machine tools: Power-driven machines that shape, cut, or grind materials such as metal, and accurately make finished parts.

militia: A group of citizens who are trained as soldiers but do not form part of the regular military. State militia members could be called out to help to defend the state in times of emergency.

mill village: A settlement built by a manufacturing company to house its workers. Whitneyville was the first mill village to be built in the United States.

Ordnance Department: A governmental department created in May 1812 to deal with military weapons, ammunition, and related equipment.

piracy: Using another person's invention for private purposes, without authorization.

trip-hammer: A weighty, power-driven hammer used in factories. It is raised by means of an unevenly shaped disc or cylinder, called a cam, and then allowed to fall by force of gravity.

yellow fever: A very infectious tropical disease that is transmitted when a person is bitten by an infected mosquito. There is no treatment, and 5 to 10 percent of people who catch yellow fever die of the disease. Nowadays there is a vaccination for yellow fever, but in the past, outbreaks were common. They often occurred when an infected traveler arrived by ship at a harbor town.

FOR MORE INFORMATION

BOOKS

Judith Alter, *Eli Whitney*. New York: Franklin Watts, 1990.

Constance M.L. Green, *Eli Whitney and the Birth of American Technology*. Boston: Little, Brown, 1956.

Anita Louise McCormick, *The Industrial Revolution in American History*. Springfield, NJ: Enslow, 1998.

Denison Olmsted, *Memoir of Eli Whitney, Esq. 1846*. Reprint, New York: Arno, 1972.

WEBSITE

Eli Whitney Museum
www.eliwhitney.org
Learn more about the machines that Eli Whitney invented. To read about Whitney's factory and how his work changed America, click on "Exhibits" and then "Inventing Change."

INDEX